M000316271

FJORDS vol.II

also by Zachary Schomburg

Pulver Maar (2019)
The Book of Joshua (2014)
Fjords vol.1 (2012)
Scary, No Scary (2009)
The Man Suit (2007)

Fjords vol. 2

by Zachary Schomburg

Black Ocean
Boston - Chicago

Copyright © 2021 by Zachary Schomburg
All rights reserved.

To reprint, reproduce, or transmit electronically, or by recording all or part of this manuscript, beyond brief reviews or educational purposes, please send a written request to the publisher at:

Black Ocean
P.O. Box 52030
Boston, MA 02205
blackocean.org

Cover Art and Design by Denny Schmickle
Book Design by Janaka Stucky

ISBN 978-1-939568-37-3

Library of Congress Control Number: 2021007549

FIRST EDITION

TABLE OF CONTENTS

WHAT WOULD KILL ME

On page 63 of my copy of *Woman in the Dunes* by Kobo Abe, someone had underlined "A monotonous existence enclosed in an eye." How much sand there is depends on how far away you are from the sand, I thought. A spot. The whole sky. A week later, while watching Teshigahara's 1964 film, I paused it at 1:40:58 when I got up to get another cold drink. It was a hot night. There were no screens on my windows. Right there in front of me, three men stood still on a sand dune with flashlights in the dark. Together, they looked like the bright unblinking eyes of a jumping spider. I can not stop, I thought, the spider, or a pursuit, or from tiring in quicksand, or a madness in the darkness, or a tiny light-pink fruit fly, the hot breath of a bear, an always on television, from finding a pair of scissors on the moon, or when I die, noticing my death notice me.

SUNA NO ONNA

A dune is a lot like a fjord. They move so slowly you can't see them move, and they have many small things in them, like saw beetles, or woodbores. When the darkness falls, and no one is around, they talk to each other very quietly. Fjords to other fjords, dunes to other dunes. Like I said, there's little difference. I'm a fjord, says a fjord. I'm a dune, says a dune. Their lives are lived proving their nature without the proper certification. I am a true dune, I am a true fjord, and how I long only to be a dune, and how I long only to be a fjord. You think it's easy to be sealed up inside yourself, like a person inside a person, holding onto your secret name like your last glass of water? Look at you go, how you go to your own funeral forever.

THIS IS THE LIFE

We were folding our clothes in the laundry room when Rita looked out the window. "This is the life," she said. "Yes, it sure is," I said with a little laugh. "Yes, this is the life," she said again. A pair of pants hung still in her hands. "Do you see something moving in the bush?" I only wanted her to snap back. We had a lot of clothes left to fold. "Rita? Is everything ok?" "The life," she said, looking squarely at the bush. I looked more closely at it too. It was, in fact, moving. Not moving in the wind, but moving away, sliding slowly toward the trees on the other side of the lawn. All afternoon, we watched it go, past the trees, a speck in the setting sun. Then the trees, too, started to move, and move slowly away, into the sun. Then our one-car garage, and the neighbor's garage, and then the neighbor's house. We didn't even know them. We wanted to introduce ourselves, but we never got around to it. There was nothing left on our lawn but long shadows and no way of knowing what made them. "We used to drape it in electric bulbs," Rita said, returning to the folding. But that was a different life.

THESE DAYS

These days, I'm so far behind. I do some things to catch up, but catching up only reminds me of all the things I'm not doing, the things I still need to do. So I put the things I need to do into three categories. One is what needs to be sold for cake. My mother only eats cake for dinner. I caught her once, in the middle of the night, slumped over the dinner table with cake all over her face and in her hair. She growled at me like a hurt cat. Another is to count how many things are on other things. How many needles are on this tree. I don't know where to begin counting. And I don't know where to end. The wind is always changing, taking needles with it. The world is changing in every way, every second. And that is the third thing. I have had access to electricity all my life, and still, I am here.

DURANGO, COLORADO

In Durango, Colorado, there is no electricity. The streets at night are the streets of an old planet. The night there just hurls itself across the plains of the universe. Everyone there wears white. Everyone there is named Estaban too, the brightest of all the names. You can really see Esteban amongst the blackness, a big moon in and of herself. But not glowing, or shining. More like a peeled potato in a black paper sack. "Hello there, Esteban!" you yell. Esteban squints and looks around for a few seconds down the dark impossible streets of Durango. You even see her sniffing like a hound. You're only a visitor here. You know that. But can you feel it, how you're giving life a try?

INFLATABLE BARBEQUE CART

When I arrived home from work, there was a man wearing a paper chicken on his head standing in my front yard. He unfolded a box that popped up quickly into an inflatable BBQ food cart. A string of lights hung down from the top of the front window, and he strung them along the outside. "Excuse me," I said. "This is my lawn." The man kept stringing the lights. "It's ok. This won't take long," he said. Inside the cart, the rotisserie machines slowly spun. Some chickens glistened. "But my wife," I said. "She'll be home any minute." To that, the man with the paper chicken head smiled. "It's ok," he reassured me. "This won't take long." And he was right. I remember nothing after that, only the speed at which it happened.

NOT REAL OR AFRAID

Hearing a fly making a life in a box means nothing but how will I get by now. I am not the only one in this life. You, for example, are also in this life. More specifically, we are on the same airplane in this life. What is flying if not a chance to end it all gracefully. One vibration is all it would take. A little buzzing is all it would take. A fly dying on my eye. I, heavily, with a fucked heart mouth it's showtime.

ICELAND

My mother and I were on a horse. We were going to a funeral. It doesn't matter whose, but it was an important funeral, a public figure. My mother was weeping. I was four. We were on an island called Iceland. The thing about the horses there is you have to sit on them sideways. They do not get diseases. Many of them are born on the outside. They carry the midwife to and from the birth. And you can't name them some bullshit name like Yogurt.

CONTINUITY OF PARKS

I was reading a story by Cortazar called "Continuity of Parks" while sitting on a bench in the park near a few wild parrots pecking at a dropped ice cream cone. In the story, a man was sitting in his favorite green chair reading a novel with great intensity as he neared the end. In the novel he was reading, a woman was plotting to murder her lover with a dagger. As she approached her lover from behind, there he was, sitting in his green chair, reading a novel about a man about to be killed from behind while sitting in his green chair. Before killing him, the woman leaned carefully and quietly in, then read a few sentences over his shoulder. There she was, in the novel he was reading, behind his green chair, dagger in hand, about to kill him. But instead of killing him, she was reading. Now everyone is reading. The killer is reading. The man is reading. And me. I am reading. Even you are reading. We are all here reading in this book together.

THE CLIFF FLOATS LOW

Two nuns are on a cliff looking at a cloud over another cliff. "It looks like a crown, but on what head," one said. "It looks like a cliff," said the other. "But that is a cliff," said the first nun. "No, the cloud," said the other nun. "The cloud looks like a cliff?" asked the first. "Yeah," said the other. And she was right. The cloud did look like a cliff floating low above the cliff. And in that, the cloud was a cliff. Because what is a cliff if not something that looks like a cliff? And this nun's cliff, a cliff set free finally from its valley, after a million years or more, like the splintered breath of a sick planet. The cliff, she thought, is going nowhere and everywhere at once. "I want to be on it," she said, weeping now. It looked like it was being held on a string. She thought of the last time she was so properly held, when she felt as light as this cliff, in the arms of her mother, and how her mother leaned down to kiss her bright red child-ears and whispered, "You feel like nothing."

FALLING FOR A BEAM OF LIGHT

I was asleep on the floor in the middle of the room, in the middle of the day, when I was awoken by a beam of light. It came in from the window across my arms and it lay there. Everything is going to be ok, I thought. It's just going to be the two of us now.

THE PURSUED ARE BEAUTIFUL

It's the pursued who always tire faster. They know how it will end, and knowing adds a weight to be carried on the back. It always ends in the quicksand. There, there is no floor. How terrible to fight inside a life with no floor. But what is truly terrible is what's above, which is nothing. We sink away from nothing. It looks for a second like a soft blue flower teetering on the tip of a wet red finger.

PLANTS

Plants are colder than you think. You need to warm them up. You can put them near the heat. Have you ever showered with your plant? Stand there with it in your arms, the light from the shower window pushing through the steam, in your hot wet bathroom in the middle of some afternoon? Wipe the steam with your finger. Look out at all the people living a life. Moving around between things, hardly touching anything. They go to the zoo. They make wishes.

INSIDE THE TIGER

Just like that, I was inside the tiger. But for the first time in a long time, I felt like I was a part of something bigger than myself, a bigger tiger. As it hunted, I hunted. We are in the tree, silent as a cloud on the long branch above our prey, a deer, my deer too, when it opened its mouth, and just like that, the deer was in my lap, twisted up, sobbing into a soft corner patch of hair, like the soft hair on the head of a baby. Together, we will be carried forever, through this death, a hole through which to fail this life straight through. How I would say thank you so sincerely from this mouth would kill us all. Thank you.

A CASE FOR HOLDING

You were treading water on your back in the middle of
a swimming pool in the desert. No one else was around.
No lifeguards or other swimmers. No coyotes in the
mountains. No hawks on the cacti. The air was light and
silent. The sun was going down. It had been a long day.
Below the surface, you looked up to see a little shadow
on the pool wall. When you came up, there was a girl.
"I didn't see you there," you said. She didn't notice you.
You swam over to her. "I didn't see you there," you said
again, putting your hand on the edge of the pool beside
her. Another girl appeared, then sat right where you had
put your hand. "Excuse me," you said. The girls giggled.
They looked like sisters. They were both wearing long
pink dresses with yellow ducks. "Are you sisters?" you
asked. You put your hand on the edge of the pool, but
as soon as you did, a third girl appeared, pink dress,
yellow ducks, and sat right where you had put your
hand. "Are you sisters?" you asked, treading water. The
three of them smiled. They would tell you if they could,
you thought. You swam across to the other side of the
pool to get some rest on the edge. But then another girl
appeared just before you could put your hand there. And
then another. Dress. Ducks. "Are you all sisters?" you
asked, treading, treading. A big cloud comes nimbly in
weighing 1.1 million pounds.

FEEL THE FALCON

I feel the falcon on the mountain. It picks me, points right at me with its one claw. Caw caw. A hollow love, a hollow flow of love, a light box of love on a cloud. It's how I know I'm me. Please, someone, land in my room. I will make great art. I will make a great piece of art. I will make a great set of choices forever. Here's my first one: one hook of joy.

POEM ABOUT ZENO

I wanted to write a poem about Zeno, who was a boy from Mexico pictured in a photograph in an old book of Mexican food recipes. The photograph was supposed to give some context. It looked like he was afraid of a ghost that was right behind him. He was afraid of ghosts, thinking now, only for a second, for less than a second, for whatever amount of time lapses in one flash, for all I know. I don't know anything. I don't know where that book went, but I remember where I was standing when I looked at it. I was beneath a tree that carried its leaves like its only thousands of babies.

CHARLES, THE BORING LAKE

There once was a boring lake named Charles. It lived in Canada, just southeast of the Northwest Terrirorities. It was one of 13 other lakes in Canada named Charles, but it didn't mind at all! It had some trout in it. It liked a cold rain on its small waves. It liked to listen to the gulping kuk-kuk-kuks of the pied billed grebes.

LAND OF THE FREE

I was busy eating a butterscotch candy next to my pony
when my tote bag was found. "Your tote bag!" shouted
someone named Land of the Free. "I found it." He was
fast-walking toward me waving the tote bag from side to
side in the air. "Where did you find it?" I said. He looked
disappointed. "Down there," he said, pointing nowhere
in particular. "Down where?" I said. "Where you left it,"
he said. This was clearly going nowhere. "How did you
know I was missing a tote bag?" I said. "I saw you earlier,"
he said. "It hung from your shoulder perfectly at your
hips, right at hip level, as you rode your pony expertly,"
he said. We both were quiet for a moment. Then he
put his hand out, "Hey there, I'm Land of the Free," he
said. "I know who you are," I said. "How?" he said. His
question pushed me off balance. "From before," I said.
"When before?" he said. It didn't matter, and I'll always
regret what happened next. I've only ever wanted to be
gone, I explained to him, more or less, like a lightness,
like light air rising in the other air, riding my pony over
an ocean of many balls of yarn, and then finally arriving
at a forest made of many balls of yarn, and riding into it.

WILD SWAN

Like a wild swan with a blue shadow, I know not where
I've swum. I bow down my head deep in the dark ripple.
I honk there deep into the darkness. I have nothing to
lose and something to prove. Two identical feelings. One
is how long is grief gone. One is when will it come back.

LITTLE BY LITTLE WE STOP THINKING

My father was on top of my brother, his knees on my brother's arms. He looked like a toppling house on top of another house just starting to topple. The house he looked like flew across the sky like a box kite in a storm. I was watching all this from who knows how far away. A few feet? A mile? A year? A hundred of something? From across the wild and out of control river? From the garden I'm gardening and bound to die upon? I don't even know these people. I do not recognize them. But I do want more than anything a third house to think about, a bigger one, to come down on it all, to kill every light I've ever turned on, to pin me with the pitiless weight of true love.

HORSE COW

One thing about horse cows is they have big hearts. They love you, and they will carry that love for you into a boiling river. They will carry you to an important funeral in Svalbard over the mountains of Hraundrangito. I once knew the love of a horse cow. It was a silent time, a time of low light. We took off together our clothes.

THIS THEY'LL SAY
SERVES YOU RIGHTLY

She chopped with apathy the arugula and endive. She topped it with crumbs, macadamia, sherry, avocado. She grabbed the beef in her hands. She chopped at it a little. She set the table. She sat at it. She ate at it. What will they say? At the end, what will they say? She put all that remained away.

FLUSHING MICHIGAN

We eat a hot dog on the bow of a cruise ship. It was where Flushing Michigan once was—one long long flat wave. I think of a noise inside of another noise, the water on the sea. "What did I do to deserve this," you say. The hot dog is so beautiful you get choked up. "Maybe just lick it," I say. Who among us can put our body in the light, and not light up?

FEELING BEING ALIVE

I babysat for a family with two children who lived on the end of the cul-de-sac in a neighborhood of cul-de-sacs. I remember how bored and disappointed the children seemed upon my arrival, so I taught them how to climb onto their own roof. The danger perked us all up. It was a steep roof. A two story house. Or was it three? We uncautiously played a game called Help Help. The three of us, tired from hours of laughing into the face of certain death, sat still on the roof, looking out over all the other rooftops, a sea of other cul-de-sacs, ones even they had never before known. What a place to live, we each thought, above a life. When the parents returned home, they had to help lower their own children down to safety, back into the life. "In the dark, no less," said the parents, incredulously. "Only now has it become dark," I said.

STUD OF THE YEAR

On your way to the hotel, someone calls out, "Hey, aren't you the Stud of the Year?" "Excuse me?" you say. "Yeah, it's you alright, you're the Stud of the Year," he says. "You must be mistaken," you say. A small crowd begins to form around you. "Hey, it's the Stud of the Year!" says someone else. "Look, I'm not the Stud of the Year," you say somewhat under your breath. You don't mean to embarass anyone. One man, upon looking at you, faints, but no one else seems to notice or care. They just keep pointing at you. You push your way over to the fainted. "Are you ok?" you say, helping him up. "I'm fine," he says, coming to. Seeing this act of heroism, a few others in the crowd faint. "Oh dear," you say, going around to each of the newly fainted in the order in which their fainting occured, asking each of them if they are ok, and helping each of them up. This causes a stirring, and much more fainting occurs. Soon, the whole city is passed out, day turns into night, the street lamps come on, a trampled field of daffodils.

LAY DOWN LITTLE TROUBLES

I scoop up different kinds of shit in the desert with a shovel, but the shovel is much too big. I can hardly lift it, even when it is empty. It's made of lead. It's the size of a saguaro cactus. I lift the handle with all the strength I can muster in my whole body, and I plunge and plunge. But it's no use. There are piles of shit everywhere. Every night, same as tonight, cold and quiet, I lean my big big shovel on my house and I go inside to bed. People are good, I say. Horses are prancing evenly. Look at the moon, and never look away until the moon looks back. Otherwise, we are lost.

REAL NICE ELKS

The people I know know some real nice elks. The nice elks they know know no pain. They are the kind of elks that have hands that only close to open. All day they hold. All day they rub. When you're a real nice elk, you're a real nice elk forever. Then your long neck floats down to the mud just because, because at the end, there's only one way of going away, a long way, along a long darkness too nice not to love.

THE CRUSHING PAIN OF EXISTENCE

My dad had a favorite spoon. Before each meal, he'd shuffle the little stack and pick it out from the drawer. He'd push his thumb into it and rub it around. It was smaller than the other spoons, and a different shape. It fit into his mouth better, he'd say. I lived only to see how long I could outlive him, how long I could carry it for. Then one day I lost it. Morning came again, and again, and again. I love you is a wish.

HUNDREDS OF YEARS OF DEATH

We were on our way to the funeral. I cried so hard, I became a horse. Then just like that, I was a dead horse. And then again, just like that, I'd been a horse dead for years. No one, even those who'd rode me, remembered me. But I was happy, dead. Hundreds of years of death. A black hole of years of death. Joy is a surprise. It can only happen once, and it can only come from nowhere. Like how this is not the end of a poem.

YOUR PAIN IS NOT ENOUGH

My dad and I were playing softball in the park when a family wearing long black robes showed up. They stood on the first baseline. "Hey, can we play ball?" they said. Their voice sounded like an old organ. "Sorry," I said. "It's just me and my dad." "It's ok," they said. "We get it." My dad lobbed the ball to me from the mound. I could tell he wanted to just keep things moving. The family in long black robes felt heavy, even at that distance, like a thousand tons of sorrow. Their sorrow dimmed the sun. My dad's pitch was perfect, right down the middle, but I just didn't have the heart to swing at it. "Why didn't you swing?" said the family. "It was right down the middle." They were right. I had no excuses. I lost a light, all feeling, maybe forever. How else to say this? Dad? I had no blood. I had no blood. My blood bled, but I did not bleed blood.

HOW THE STRAWBERRY IS HELD

I like the way the robot holds the strawberry in its hand and how it uses just the two digits it needs to hold it. They come together like a curtain from both sides of a stage, and not like two iron walls cutting through the choppy grey sea to close a canal. To hold it like that takes the right amount of squeeze, enough so as not to drop it, but not so much so as to crush it. I like the way, too, how the bird flits politely down onto the robot's other hand wanting to eat.

INVADERS NEVER WANDER

I was working the ticket booth of a movie theater in Laredo when management showed up unexpectedly one night. They said we had been going through more popcorn than what the sales reports indicated, and they wanted to know who'd been eating all the popcorn. There were three of them wearing FBI-looking suits. "Do you want some popcorn?" I said. They took me into the back room. "This isn't a joke," one of them said. "It isn't a charity either," said another. "And it's also not a free-for-all," added the third. "Well, then what could it be?" I said. "Those are the only three things." "What are the only three things?" said the first one. "Like you said— jokes, charity, and free-for-alls," I said. "I can't think of another thing that things like this are. Can you?" They each started thinking of a good fourth thing that things like this are. There were a few moments where we all thought they had thought of something, a good fourth thing, but then they didn't have anything, or at least they weren't ready to share it. I thought of a few fourth things, but I kept them to myself. Poltergeist II had just been let out, and I could hear people gather their coats, and walk back through the lobby, back out to their parked cars. I thought about them going home to eat ice cream, living a whole life in a few different mid-sized homes, having manners, looking at Wife on gravestones.

SADDER SUMMER

The house was crumbling down slowly around me like a paper marigold. It had been a summer full of interviews. I had become simplified into my most primitive body. Now me experienced, me said. Now me not alone.

AFRAID CLOUD

My father left his horse at my house. He wanted me to fix it, but it died right away. Preserve the head, I remember him once telling me, was something to do after a horse dies. Bury the head. But it was too much, the blood, the weight of even one leg, the too-small bags. I never told my father about his horse, and he never asked. It never came up. If death has a start, it also has an end. Afraid cloud, I don't remember you.

JOKE ABOUT HAMBURGERS

Two hamburgers walk into a bar. That's how my joke started. I was 6, or maybe 7 or 8. I remember climbing up a stone wall to tell it, and how I thought on the other side there'd be cows to tell it to, but there were no cows. Then I fell into the field on the other side of the stone wall. On my back, in the dirt, I pretended I was dead. I heard my grandmother ask my mom where I was, and my mom asked my sister. They all got into a car. I don't even remember how it went.

GIVE A KITE TAKE A KITE

I started a Give-a-Kite-Take-a-Kite program at work. Everyone was stressed about the big project, so it was the least I could do. I thought about all the different box kites dancing against the sky over the tree tops. But no one ever used it. It was just a waste paper basket in the corner. One day, I saw a frog in it.

ON KILLING

It takes about 100 generations of mice to build up a tolerance for all the stings to the face a scorpion delivers. They take the blow, and then they know they're not the one. But then comes along a mouse that can take it. It goes into the den. Its body blocks the pain. The thing about killing is, like everything else, it feels as bright as love for just a flash.

LOOK AT THAT CLOUD

I hear some claws on the screen door. Is it the dog going in, or going out? The cloud moves in slow, like a rabbit, like a dying rabbit, like a dead rabbit. I get a letter from myself at five. I write myself at five back. I include a picture and a little note. Here's you wearing a big cowboy hat.

THE GOLDEN YEARS

From this darker center someone must care for me like
a father in the strawberries, but I do not love you, not
like he tends them. We live beneath the clouds where all
things not clouds go bad.

GLASS TO GLASS

My friend had an imaginary friend named Erker, and when I brought it up to him, he had no memory of it. I told my mom about Erker, and how my friend didn't remember, but my mom didn't remember my friend. "Are you speaking of your imaginary friend, Glass to Glass?" she said. But I had no memory of Glass to Glass. "He was a bear," she said.

NO GOING BACK

I thought we were at the turnoff, but we were nowhere, when the ghost rears with its red edge, a ghost of a ghost of something fanged, its fang jutting at us all, a wild judge, growing faster every day, like a moutain, on the top of which we deflower a flower, there's no stopping nothing now, no killing the killed, no more having, so we take it, a needle piercing an ice shelf until it calves.

A MONOTONOUS EXISTENCE ENCLOSED IN AN EYE

"Fuck, yeah!" I said. I was so far gone. I felt like I could see all of time all at once. I was haunting myself from the future. "Fuck, yeah!" I said again. I was wild in the wild meadow. I was absolutely out of control. It was the first time in my life that my fate was held truly in my own hands. Hold my fate, buttercup. Hold my fate like a buttercup.

TO BEAR IS BORING

Someone named Hurt Swan came over to my house to use the bathroom. "It was ok," I thought, just Hurt Swan. But after he washed up and left, another person came over, and politely asked to use the bathroom. "Hurt Swan said you had a bathroom I could use," she said. "Yes," I said, "but it's not for just anyone." "What are you saying?" she said, and she makes a good point. An hour or so later, a third person dropped by. "You have a bathroom?" he said. "Yeah," I said. In no time, there was a line around the block, trampling my neighbor's squash garden. I yelled to the back of the line, "It'll be a few minutes, please be patient." The wait was too long, and people were starting to complain. I understood the problem, so I started a sign up sheet so people wouldn't have to wait in the line. "I'll call you when it's your turn," I said to everyone. That worked for a while, but there was just no catching up, no end in sight, and still so many people had to go to the bathroom. That's when Hurt Swan came back. "Hey, I have to go again," he said. "But the wait is too long." He looked like he was in pain. The thing is, I knew what it was like to have to go to the bathroom that bad. "I have another bathroom," I whispered. "It's upstairs, take a right down the hallway, and then another right down another hallway, and then another right, and another right and another and another." May you all live forever.

HAIRCUTS OF ICEBERGS

A long time ago, the icebergs all had haircuts. They bopped around the young sea, each with a different haircut, big poofy ones, ones parted in the middle. "Nice hair," is how icebergs would greet each other, every few thousand years, when they'd near. Once they all melted, the sea was never the same, and their haircuts washed up on the beaches like perfect gifts for the tops of heads of people, but it turned out we were much too small.

HOW I'M A GREAT PAINTER

There was an ant as big as a couch crawling all over everything. It was eating my mom's favorite chair. I whacked it with my bat, and it opened like a hard loaf of sourdough. It was so blue inside, and the blue went everywhere. Into every crack. Into my ideas. Even my eyes as they look out at the trees. Now I only paint with one color. This is how I'm a great painter.

LEG ENTRANCE

Above the door, there is a sign that reads, Leg Entrance. When I tried to walk through, I was stopped by a leg. "Legs only," it said. "But I'm with them," I said, pointing to my own two legs. "I'm sorry," said the leg, pointing to the sign. There was no use in arguing. There's nothing I could do. I walked around outside until I found a wall, then I sat on the wall and looked at my legs. They looked so far away. They looked like nothing else I had ever known. They looked like two hot dogs. I wanted to hold them like I loved them because, for the first time, in that moment, I did. If I could, I would. I would love anything and anyone. I would hover lovingly over all of your houses.

HELP HELP

Some people say our planet is a tiny baby, and the mountains are pores on the baby's eyes. I squint to see it, then Stars for Eyes puts the baby in my arms. I'm the mother now. "There's no going back," I whispered to my baby. "You're my love," I whisper. And when I drop it, it never hits the ground.

LUCKY DONKEY

I used to know a very lucky donkey. It got everything it ever wanted. It spent its days standing in the sun, eating strawberries from a good bush. One day, I asked it for its secrets. "You have to bray for what you want," it said. Then it got on its knees and brayed. Just then, another good bush appeared. "Here's your good bush," it said. But who needs a good bush, I thought, when you got a lucky donkey.

KIND OF MAN

I am the kind of man who keeps his eyes closed for days, walks into things, falls into holes, touches people he knows and loves faces. I once held a bat in my fist, the one to come screaming out of a tunnel. There's only one that lights the way, so to speak, for the others. That bat that lights bit me, and now I am a bat. I am a man, but I am also a bat. It's nothing like what you're thinking. Spare me the joke. Besides, the days of tunneling through the blacknesses of a life are behind me. These days, I do things right. I count the potatoes, I get in line for a good haircut. The kind of life one lives in a house. The kind of house that fits perfectly around its key. Just not this key.

ROAD SAFETY

Before you cross the street, be sure to look both ways. It's very important. Stop at stop signs. Just, generally, be confident, and don't be in a hurry. When you're driving, do not stop for pedestrians unless there is a crosswalk. Stopping seems polite, but it puts that pedestrian in danger. Leave plenty of room between yourself and other vehicles. Remember, everyone is trying to kill you. Don't be afraid. Always use your mirrors and your turn signal.

SEA LION CAVES MUG

Someone at work stole my Sea Lion Caves mug. It was Japanese stonewear, and I remember its blue waves and its orange sun. I remember its lighthouse and its seabirds. I'd never before been to the Sea Lion Caves. I've never been anywhere near them. But if I could, I'd go so deep, into the deepest depths, where there is no scratch of light left on my eye, and where there is no sound. I would only hear my heart, and it would pound out a beautiful song that goes you know not what you've done you know not what you've done.

WHOSE BEAUTY IS TOMBIER

Because a very tall bookshelf had fallen on you, I wanted to ease your pain. So I made you a nice painting to put on your wall. It was pink, yellow, and orange. It was of the crowns of people's heads from behind. You asked, "Are one of these my head?" I hadn't thought of it before, but I said yes, that one of them was. Later, you were run over by a silver Cadillac outside an abandoned Chinese buffet.

OLD WOOD HAIR

I was in someone named Old Wood Hair's elegant mansion eating dinner when I needed to go to the bathroom. "It's down the hallway," said Old Wood Hair, but at the end of the hallway, there were no doors. Only a window. Outside of the window was a big forest. "You have a big forest!" I yelled back down the hallway. As soon as I turned around Old Wood Hair was on me. "To the right," she said. "To the right!" I felt the blood in the hole, a young sea of clothes pins washing over me.

HOW WE ARE NOTHING

We were showering in the lobby of an auto shop when the water was starting to fill up the tub part. We didn't know how to shut the water off. On the other side of the curtains, mechanics were grinding away at gears and bouncing tires. Some customers were paying. "Hey, the water is starting to fill up," we said. No one turned around. I tried again, this time projecting my voice a little more over the sound of the rushing water. "Can someone help us turn the water off?" But no one heard, or seemed to care. The soapy water started to flow over the tub part and out into the lobby. Some customers sloshed through it on their way to pick out some motor oil. We laughed so loud, the water going everywhere now. It was our chance to make a run for it, and make a run for it we did. We were neither naked or clothed. We were neither wet or dry. We never looked back. We were in love. We were nothing at all. We were less than nothing, not a fleck of something. We were not even a dot of oxygen in a tiny bush rubbing up against another tiny bush in a microscope.

DEATH TO TRAITORS

They care not what they've done. They know nothing of the world. They go nowhere on their own. They fall into the ocean. They lose your plans. When you hand them a plan, it turns to glue in their meaty hands. They only walk up the steps. They push all the buttons on the elevator. They take you to the wrong king. You can try to kill them, and you should, but they'll never die. Only when you love them will they die. And then when they are dead, they die right in front of you every night. You put their corpse on a boat in a river that's a circle. They go around how they come around.

BIEN FANG

In my backyard, while watering the row of peonies, I found a family in a house I had never noticed before. "Hey, have you been here this whole time?" I said. "We have," said the woman. "Where do you come from?" she said. "I live right there," I said, pointing to my house. "Oh, have you been there the whole time?" she said. "Yes," I said. We talked for a few hours like that, pointing at things, and asking if we've seen those things before. She picked some flowers from her yard and handed them to me. "I will miss you when you go," she said, handing me the flowers. I walked home, just a few feet away, and I dried them out between two sheets of plastic in the microwave, and then I put them between two plates of glass. I tried to look up the name of the flowers, but they weren't in any of my flower books. How strange, to go for so long in the world without a name, I thought. They looked like they had little french fangs, like a french mouth with a couple of good fangs. That's how Bien Fang came into my life, like a disappearance.

TAKE ME TO YOUR KING

When I first landed on the planet, one of them asked me what I wanted. I hadn't planned to make a statement so soon, and I was very tired. "Take me to your king," I said without thinking. "I am the king," he said. This was a great start. I killed him right away. It's important to just kill, and to not hesitate. That's something I learned when I was just a little girl. I killed everyone, and I killed everything. Love is a perfect measurement. I've come so far.

TEEN FOGS

One night, a teen fog lowered onto your head and held you down. It was on you. Face down, you felt its weight grow. Another heavier teen fog was on its head. And another teen fog was on even that teen fog. Your breath became its breath, then also its breath, and was almost gone. You are nothing, a teen fog too, a rider of teen fogs. You forgive me. You hover over me as I am face down on the lip of a frozen lake and forgive me like a great snow snowing into my hole.

POOL OF TYPIST

A few things come to mind: Hour of the Wolf, being told exactly what to do, tiring from a pursuit, death by quicksand, death by light, death by waking by mistake into a new light, modern life, adjusting the springiness of a diving board. I once wanted only to type, to type so well, to be the finest typist. I was nine. I sat in my little chair.

THE LIFE OF SOMEONE

We were all told that someone would be born on a certain day, and when that day came, almost everyone, not all, but most, were awaiting her arrival and were quite pleased when it turned out to, in fact, be her. When she died, about a hundred years later, we were all gone of course. No one was left to go to her funeral. The world was much quieter then. There were two grebes in a tree, and one even in the sea.

INDEX

NOTES on Vol. 2

The cover of the book is taken from a scene in Teshigahara's "Woman in the Dunes" (1964). "A monotonous existence enclosed in an eye" is a sentence from Kobo Abe's *A Woman in the Dunes* translated from the Japanese by E. Dale Saunders (1964). "Suna No Onna" is translated from the Japanese as "Woman in the Dunes." "These Days," "Lay Down Little Troubles," and "Whose Beauty is Tombier" takes language directly from the personal emails from Brandon Shimoda. "Pool of Typist" is for Veronica Martin. A line from "Iceland" was taken from the tour guide during a Golden Circle Classic Day Trip bustour via Gray Line. "Continuity of Parks" is a short story by Julio Cortazar from a collection called *Blow Up* (Pantheon, 1985) translated by Paul Blackburn. "Poem about Zeno" is for Brandi Herrera. "This They'll Say Serves You Rightly" is a rough translation of Edwin Madrid's "Cena." "Flushing Michigan" is for Liz Mehl. "Feeling Being Alive" is for Gary Fiscus. "Lay Down Little Troubles" ends with the last line of a speech by Adam Schiff given to congress on 2/3/20. "The Crushing Pain of Existence" is for Mathias Svalina. "Your Pain is Not Enough" is for Brandon Brown. "Invaders Never Wander" was inspired by a clip I watched of David Berman telling a story live to a crowd between songs.

"Sadder Summer" was co-written with B. "Afraid Cloud" was written for Kyle Morton. "On Killing" gets some of its information from a scene in *Night on Earth* (Netflix, 2019). "Look at that Cloud" is for my parents, Nancy and Bruce Schomburg. "Glass to Glass" is for Seth Showalter, and also for my Aunt Pam, who remembered Glass to Glass. "How I'm a Great Painter" and "How We Are Nothing" are for Kyle Vegter. "Old Wood Hair" is for Ben Niespodziany, with a title inspired by Onnovah Mains. "Death to Traitors" is for Joseph Mains. "Bien Fang" is for Katherine Herrera. "Haircuts of Icebergs" was written in response to a photograph by Adam Thorman for his Creatures Found project. "The Life of Someone" is for Connie Wilson.

ACKNOWLEDGEMENTS

Poems from Fjords v2 previously appeared in *Bodyprint*, *Columbia Poetry Review*, *Gasher*, *Gaze*, *Midst*, *Moss*, *Pulpmouth*, *Sixth Finch*, *Sublunary Editions*, and *Your Impossible Voice*. A big thanks to the editors of these journals.

THANK YOU

To B. A thank you is the absolute bare minimum, but I mean it to mean everything.

Thank you also to my mom, dad, K, J, and L. And to Janaka, Carrie, and Denny.